Reema Fairbain Wehlage

Illustrated by: Ronie Pios

Copyright © 2011 by Reema Fairbain Wehlage. 589743

To order additional copies of this book, contact:
Xlibris
844-714-8691
www.Xlibris.com
Orders@Xlibris.com

ISBN: 978-1-4653-4804-3 (sc)
ISBN: 978-1-6641-4006-6 (e)

Print information available on the last page

Rev. date: 10/28/2020

Summer time is great.

It's my favorite time of all.

We do lots of fun stuff outdoors.

My dad loves cooking on the grill when it's warm outside.

But, I love playing in my sand box with my friends.

2

In the fall, we go back to school.

We read lots of books. Reading is cool.

In the winter,
when snow covers the ground,
we must wear snow boots, our winter
coats, hats and gloves to stay warm.

Spring time is beautiful as the flowers are in bloom.

The weather is usually nice and sunny.

Easter is in the springtime.

This is when I visit my cousins.

Some of my cousins live nearby, while the rest of them

live in another country.

Did you know that some countries never experience winter?

Or even have snow? Well, some of my cousins live in such a country.

And that country is called Trinidad.

Trinidad is located in the Caribbean, just off of the coast of South America.

It has a sister island called, Tobago.

This twin - island nation is usually referred to as Trinidad and Tobago.

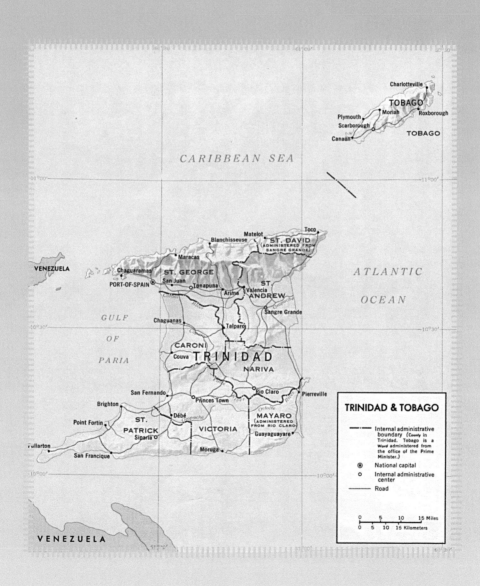

In Trinidad, as in most of the Caribbean islands, there are generally two seasons: a dry season and a wet or rainy season. The dry season is very hot, but luckily there's always a breeze.

In the rainy season, can you guess what happens?

Yep, there's lots of rain! So you'd better bring your umbrella!

The temperature can be pretty hot even in the rainy season.

Depending on how close you live to the Caribbean, you can take an airplane or a boat to get there.

Trinidad and Tobago was once governed by the Queen of England until 1962 when it became an independent nation with its own President and Prime Minister.

The Queen's Park Savannah, more commonly referred to as the Savannah, is located in the capital city of Port-of-Spain. The Savannah is one of the largest roundabouts in the world.

Stollmeyer's Castle is a beautiful building located around the Savannah. Built originally as a retirement home for an American, Charles Stollmeyer, it is now a historical building owned by the government of Trinidad and Tobago.

The steelpan is an amazing instrument played especially during the Carnival season. Carnival is similar to Mardi Gras with many different costumes worn and displayed. Calypso is the music native to Trinidad and Tobago.

The international airport is located in Piarco; which is in the north eastern part of Trinidad. Tobago has its own A.N.R. Robinson International Airport.

The population of Trinidad and Tobago is approximately 1.3 million people.

Banana

Mangoes

Cashews

Cocoa

The fruits and vegetables are somewhat different from those found in temperate climates. Fruits found in warmer climates are usually referred to as Tropical fruits.

Some fruits common to Trinidad and Tobago are:

Mango

Passion fruit

Cashew

pineapple

Guava

Plum

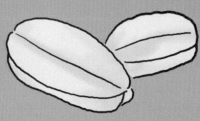

Five finger

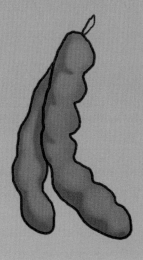

Tamarind

Chenette fruit

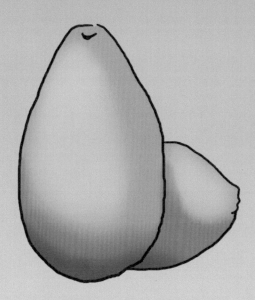

Pomme cythere

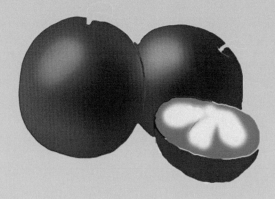

Caimit

Cherries

Banana

Coconut

While the mature or dried coconut is used for cooking and baking. The water inside the young coconut is a very refreshing drink. The young coconut also contains a soft, edible and very delicious jelly. On any given evening, you can enjoy a cool drink of coconut water around the Queen's Park Savannah.

The food is a myriad of all the different cultures and nationalities that once inhabited the islands. Some of these cultures include: English, French, African, East Indian, Amerindian, Spanish and Chinese.

Roti and pelau are traditional dishes. Roti is a flat-bread made with flour and split peas. Once cooked, it's wrapped with meat, potatoes, vegetables or whatever your taste buds desire. Pelau consists of rice cooked with meat, peas and a blend of spices.

Two major sports played in Trinidad are: football which is also called soccer and cricket.

Have you played cricket before?

Cricket is a game that requires a bat and a ball. These are quite different from the ones used in baseball. The winning team is the one scoring the highest number of runs in the allotted time.

In the past, during professional cricket matches, all players wore white uniforms. But nowadays, teams wear many different color uniforms.

Brian Lara of Trinidad and Sir Vivian Richards of Antigua are regarded among the best batsmen ever to have played the game of cricket.

Brian Lara

The cool Caribbean breeze is ideal for kite flying.

My favorite thing to do in Trinidad is going to the beach. There are many beautiful beaches in Trinidad and Tobago. But, my favorite beach of all is Maracas Bay.

I build sand castles and skip on the waves.

At Maracas Bay, a man named Richard sells
bake and shark. I love these bakes, they are
so delicious. There are other vendors who
sell jewelry and handbags made from local
materials such as coconut and calabash.

On some beaches, early in the morning, you can see fishermen hauling in their nets filled with many fishes.

When my vacation is over, I say good-bye to my cousins. Then board a plane with my mom and dad and together we fly home......

...back to playing in my sand box with my friends.